AF413638

TWO-STEP PROBLEMS FOR 2ND GRADERS

Math Books for Kids
Children's Math Books

Speedy Publishing LLC

40 E. Main St. #1156

Newark, DE 19711

www.speedypublishing.com

Copyright 2017

Solve each
two-step problem.
Write the solution in
the space provided.

EXERCISE NO. 1

Solve each equation.
Write the solution in the space provided.

(1) $8 - 4 + 10 =$

(2) $10 - 7 + 10 =$

(3) $8 + 5 + 5 =$

(4) $8 - 4 - 2 =$

(5) $10 + 8 - 6 =$

(6) $6 + 9 + 9 =$

(7) $9 - 5 - 3 =$

(8) $5 - 4 + 2 =$

(9) $6 - 3 + 8 =$

(10) $7 - 2 - 2 =$

EXERCISE NO. 2

Solve each equation.
Write the solution in the space provided.

(1) $10 - 9 + 3 \;=$

(2) $9 + 2 + 5 \;=$

(3) $9 - 6 + 7 \;=$

(4) $9 + 2 - 8 \;=$

(5) $5 - 3 + 10 \;=$

(6) $6 + 5 - 6 \;=$

(7) $7 + 8 + 5 \;=$

(8) $6 - 2 + 9 \;=$

(9) $5 + 9 + 10 \;=$

(10) $9 - 2 + 9 \;=$

EXERCISE NO. 3

Solve each equation.
Write the solution in the space provided.

(1) $9 - 4 - 3 =$

(2) $5 - 3 + 6 =$

(3) $3 + 6 + 4 =$

(4) $9 - 4 + 10 =$

(5) $10 - 8 + 9 =$

(6) $2 + 10 - 4 =$

(7) $10 - 5 + 8 =$

(8) $9 - 6 + 6 =$

(9) $5 + 3 + 5 =$

(10) $5 - 2 + 8 =$

EXERCISE NO. 4

Solve each equation.
Write the solution in the space provided.

(1) $8 + 8 - 8 =$

(2) $9 - 4 + 5 =$

(3) $8 - 2 + 8 =$

(4) $9 - 8 + 8 =$

(5) $5 + 7 - 2 =$

(6) $7 - 6 + 2 =$

(7) $3 + 9 + 4 =$

(8) $10 - 3 - 4 =$

(9) $6 - 4 + 5 =$

(10) $4 + 6 + 10 =$

EXERCISE NO. 5

Solve each equation.
Write the solution in the space provided.

(1) $6 + 3 - 2 \ =$

(2) $9 - 5 + 10 \ =$

(3) $10 + 4 - 7 \ =$

(4) $7 - 3 + 4 \ =$

(5) $9 - 2 + 9 \ =$

(6) $2 + 7 - 4 \ =$

(7) $10 - 4 + 2 \ =$

(8) $4 - 2 + 7 \ =$

(9) $4 + 9 - 4 \ =$

(10) $3 + 7 - 2 \ =$

EXERCISE NO. 6

Solve each equation.
Write the solution in the space provided.

(1) $7 - 4 + 7 \ =$

(2) $9 + 4 + 10 \ =$

(3) $9 + 4 - 8 \ =$

(4) $8 + 3 - 6 \ =$

(5) $3 - 2 + 2 \ =$

(6) $8 - 6 + 10 \ =$

(7) $10 + 6 - 4 \ =$

(8) $10 - 9 + 2 \ =$

(9) $8 - 4 + 7 \ =$

(10) $10 + 6 + 7 \ =$

EXERCISE NO. 7

Solve each equation.
Write the solution in the space provided.

(1) $9 - 2 - 5 =$

(2) $5 + 5 + 2 =$

(3) $9 + 9 - 6 =$

(4) $10 + 4 - 5 =$

(5) $7 + 3 + 5 =$

(6) $2 + 10 - 10 =$

(7) $6 - 3 + 10 =$

(8) $8 - 3 - 4 =$

(9) $3 + 6 - 5 =$

(10) $4 - 2 + 3 =$

EXERCISE NO. 8

Solve each equation.
Write the solution in the space provided.

(1) $9 + 8 + 9 =$

(2) $5 + 9 - 3 =$

(3) $6 - 4 + 2 =$

(4) $5 - 2 + 10 =$

(5) $4 + 6 - 4 =$

(6) $6 + 5 + 10 =$

(7) $8 + 2 - 4 =$

(8) $8 - 4 + 2 =$

(9) $7 + 7 - 2 =$

(10) $5 + 9 + 8 =$

EXERCISE NO. 9

Solve each equation.
Write the solution in the space provided.

(1) $5 + 10 + 7 =$

(2) $2 + 6 + 4 =$

(3) $3 + 3 + 6 =$

(4) $6 + 4 - 6 =$

(5) $8 + 6 - 3 =$

(6) $8 - 7 + 7 =$

(7) $8 + 7 + 6 =$

(8) $8 + 7 - 6 =$

(9) $3 + 3 - 5 =$

(10) $4 + 5 + 5 =$

EXERCISE NO. 10

Solve each equation.
Write the solution in the space provided.

(1) $6 + 3 - 5 \;=$

(2) $3 + 2 + 6 \;=$

(3) $10 - 4 + 4 \;=$

(4) $5 + 6 + 7 \;=$

(5) $5 + 6 - 7 \;=$

(6) $2 + 4 - 4 \;=$

(7) $10 + 7 + 3 \;=$

(8) $9 + 9 - 9 \;=$

(9) $10 - 4 + 10 \;=$

(10) $7 + 8 + 9 \;=$

EXERCISE NO. 11

Solve each equation.
Write the solution in the space provided.

(1) $7 \times 4 + 10 \ =$

(2) $5 \times 10 + 8 \ =$

(3) $2 \times 9 + 8 \ =$

(4) $5 \times 10 - 7 \ =$

(5) $7 \times 4 - 10 \ =$

(6) $6 \times 8 - 5 \ =$

(7) $10 \times 5 + 8 \ =$

(8) $10 \times 5 - 8 \ =$

(9) $2 \times 9 - 6 \ =$

(10) $3 \times 2 + 2 \ =$

EXERCISE NO. 12

Solve each equation.
Write the solution in the space provided.

(1) $9 \times 8 + 4 =$

(2) $9 \times 6 + 9 =$

(3) $6 \times 9 - 8 =$

(4) $2 \times 5 + 3 =$

(5) $10 \times 7 + 8 =$

(6) $9 \times 8 - 9 =$

(7) $10 \times 7 - 2 =$

(8) $5 \times 10 + 7 =$

(9) $8 \times 6 + 2 =$

(10) $4 \times 3 - 5 =$

EXERCISE NO. 13

Solve each equation.
Write the solution in the space provided.

(1) $9 \times 4 - 6 =$

(2) $7 \times 8 - 9 =$

(3) $8 \times 5 + 4 =$

(4) $10 \times 7 + 9 =$

(5) $10 \times 7 - 2 =$

(6) $6 \times 9 - 10 =$

(7) $4 \times 6 - 2 =$

(8) $3 \times 3 - 3 =$

(9) $7 \times 8 + 7 =$

(10) $4 \times 6 + 2 =$

EXERCISE NO. 14

Solve each equation.
Write the solution in the space provided.

(1) $3 \times 7 + 6 =$

(2) $4 \times 9 + 4 =$

(3) $6 \times 4 - 10 =$

(4) $2 \times 3 + 2 =$

(5) $10 \times 2 - 9 =$

(6) $7 \times 6 - 7 =$

(7) $8 \times 5 + 7 =$

(8) $4 \times 9 - 9 =$

(9) $6 \times 8 - 8 =$

(10) $7 \times 6 + 3 =$

EXERCISE NO. 15

Solve each equation.
Write the solution in the space provided.

(1) $9 \times 5 - 9 =$

(2) $2 \times 3 - 5 =$

(3) $3 \times 4 - 9 =$

(4) $7 \times 2 - 7 =$

(5) $3 \times 4 + 6 =$

(6) $4 \times 9 - 2 =$

(7) $10 \times 5 + 10 =$

(8) $5 \times 8 - 6 =$

(9) $10 \times 5 - 2 =$

(10) $4 \times 9 + 4 =$

EXERCISE NO. 16

Solve each equation.
Write the solution in the space provided.

(1) $5 \times 5 + 4 \ =$

(2) $9 \times 3 + 8 \ =$

(3) $6 \times 8 + 3 \ =$

(4) $8 \times 4 + 4 \ =$

(5) $3 \times 9 + 6 \ =$

(6) $3 \times 9 - 9 \ =$

(7) $7 \times 6 + 9 \ =$

(8) $5 \times 7 + 3 \ =$

(9) $4 \times 10 + 3 \ =$

(10) $10 \times 2 + 3 \ =$

EXERCISE NO. 17

Solve each equation.
Write the solution in the space provided.

(1) $7 \times 2 - 9 \ =$

(2) $5 \times 3 - 4 \ =$

(3) $6 \times 10 + 8 \ =$

(4) $3 \times 5 - 10 \ =$

(5) $5 \times 10 + 8 \ =$

(6) $2 \times 4 + 5 \ =$

(7) $5 \times 3 + 6 \ =$

(8) $6 \times 10 - 7 \ =$

(9) $3 \times 5 + 10 \ =$

(10) $4 \times 6 + 5 \ =$

EXERCISE NO. 18

Solve each equation.
Write the solution in the space provided.

(1) $3 \times 10 - 3 =$

(2) $6 \times 4 + 7 =$

(3) $9 \times 6 - 10 =$

(4) $7 \times 2 + 5 =$

(5) $5 \times 3 - 5 =$

(6) $4 \times 5 + 2 =$

(7) $10 \times 9 - 6 =$

(8) $2 \times 8 + 8 =$

(9) $4 \times 5 - 7 =$

(10) $5 \times 5 + 10 =$

EXERCISE NO. 19

Solve each equation.
Write the solution in the space provided.

(1) $6 \times 8 - 7 =$

(2) $6 \times 8 + 5 =$

(3) $10 \times 7 - 3 =$

(4) $4 \times 3 + 4 =$

(5) $7 \times 9 + 2 =$

(6) $3 \times 10 + 6 =$

(7) $9 \times 4 + 5 =$

(8) $5 \times 5 + 3 =$

(9) $10 \times 7 + 7 =$

(10) $4 \times 3 - 6 =$

EXERCISE NO. 20

Solve each equation.
Write the solution in the space provided.

(1) $6 \times 3 - 2 =$

(2) $10 \times 10 + 8 =$

(3) $9 \times 2 + 9 =$

(4) $4 \times 2 + 10 =$

(5) $8 \times 4 - 7 =$

(6) $6 \times 3 + 3 =$

(7) $7 \times 5 + 6 =$

(8) $5 \times 7 - 4 =$

(9) $9 \times 2 - 7 =$

(10) $3 \times 8 - 3 =$

EXERCISE NO. 21

Solve each equation.
Write the solution in the space provided.

(1) $9 \times 4 - 8 =$

(2) $8 \times 5 - 8 =$

(3) $10 \times 2 - 7 =$

(4) $3 \times 6 - 10 =$

(5) $9 \times 4 + 8 =$

(6) $5 \times 8 - 10 =$

(7) $4 \times 7 - 7 =$

(8) $7 \times 10 - 6 =$

(9) $8 \times 5 + 7 =$

(10) $10 \times 2 + 4 =$

EXERCISE NO. 22

Solve each equation.
Write the solution in the space provided.

(1) $6 \times 10 - 9 =$

(2) $6 \times 10 + 5 =$

(3) $3 \times 2 + 10 =$

(4) $10 \times 7 - 4 =$

(5) $8 \times 4 - 2 =$

(6) $9 \times 6 + 9 =$

(7) $2 \times 9 - 3 =$

(8) $7 \times 8 + 7 =$

(9) $7 \times 8 - 7 =$

(10) $9 \times 6 - 2 =$

EXERCISE NO. 23

Solve each equation.
Write the solution in the space provided.

(1) $6 \times 5 + 10 =$

(2) $10 \times 10 + 2 =$

(3) $8 \times 2 - 5 =$

(4) $4 \times 4 + 4 =$

(5) $7 \times 9 + 9 =$

(6) $10 \times 10 - 6 =$

(7) $8 \times 2 + 5 =$

(8) $7 \times 5 + 8 =$

(9) $4 \times 4 - 3 =$

(10) $9 \times 6 + 6 =$

EXERCISE NO. 24

Solve each equation.
Write the solution in the space provided.

(1) $3 \times 8 - 10 =$

(2) $3 \times 8 + 2 =$

(3) $10 \times 5 + 2 =$

(4) $8 \times 2 + 9 =$

(5) $9 \times 10 + 3 =$

(6) $7 \times 7 + 2 =$

(7) $2 \times 9 + 5 =$

(8) $4 \times 4 + 5 =$

(9) $5 \times 3 + 5 =$

(10) $6 \times 6 + 2 =$

EXERCISE NO. 25

Solve each equation.
Write the solution in the space provided.

(1) $5 \times 9 + 2 \ =$

(2) $2 \times 2 + 7 \ =$

(3) $9 \times 6 - 10 \ =$

(4) $7 \times 3 - 7 \ =$

(5) $6 \times 10 + 7 \ =$

(6) $3 \times 8 + 3 \ =$

(7) $5 \times 9 - 9 \ =$

(8) $9 \times 6 + 4 \ =$

(9) $10 \times 4 - 4 \ =$

(10) $6 \times 10 - 5 \ =$

EXERCISE NO. 26

Solve each equation.
Write the solution in the space provided.

(1) $7 \times 6 - 4 \ =$

(2) $2 \times 2 + 6 \ =$

(3) $10 \times 7 + 10 \ =$

(4) $5 \times 5 - 9 \ =$

(5) $9 \times 4 + 9 \ =$

(6) $6 \times 9 + 9 \ =$

(7) $3 \times 8 + 5 \ =$

(8) $7 \times 6 + 2 \ =$

(9) $10 \times 7 - 6 \ =$

(10) $9 \times 4 - 7 \ =$

EXERCISE NO. 27

Solve each equation.
Write the solution in the space provided.

(1) $2 \times 6 + 4 =$

(2) $3 \times 9 + 4 =$

(3) $9 \times 8 - 7 =$

(4) $6 \times 2 + 5 =$

(5) $6 \times 2 - 9 =$

(6) $10 \times 3 + 7 =$

(7) $3 \times 9 - 9 =$

(8) $8 \times 4 + 8 =$

(9) $9 \times 8 + 4 =$

(10) $5 \times 10 + 2 =$

EXERCISE NO. 28

Solve each equation.
Write the solution in the space provided.

(1) $8 \times 10 + 6 =$

(2) $10 \times 7 - 5 =$

(3) $10 \times 7 + 3 =$

(4) $5 \times 6 + 2 =$

(5) $3 \times 3 - 3 =$

(6) $9 \times 9 - 3 =$

(7) $8 \times 10 - 3 =$

(8) $5 \times 2 - 8 =$

(9) $5 \times 2 + 5 =$

(10) $5 \times 6 - 3 =$

EXERCISE NO. 29

Solve each equation.
Write the solution in the space provided.

(1) $2 \times 8 + 10 \ =$

(2) $4 \times 7 + 4 \ =$

(3) $8 \times 2 - 9 \ =$

(4) $7 \times 5 - 6 \ =$

(5) $6 \times 10 + 4 \ =$

(6) $3 \times 4 - 2 \ =$

(7) $6 \times 3 - 6 \ =$

(8) $7 \times 5 + 3 \ =$

(9) $2 \times 8 - 4 \ =$

(10) $9 \times 6 - 2 \ =$

EXERCISE NO. 30

Solve each equation.
Write the solution in the space provided.

(1) $5 \times 8 + 5 =$

(2) $3 \times 6 + 5 =$

(3) $5 \times 8 - 9 =$

(4) $10 \times 9 - 2 =$

(5) $2 \times 7 + 7 =$

(6) $9 \times 10 + 3 =$

(7) $6 \times 4 - 5 =$

(8) $9 \times 10 - 2 =$

(9) $3 \times 6 - 3 =$

(10) $2 \times 7 - 2 =$

EXERCISE NO. 31

Solve each equation.
Write the solution in the space provided.

(1) $6 \times 10 + 6 =$

(2) $9 \times 7 - 8 =$

(3) $4 \times 9 - 7 =$

(4) $6 \times 10 - 4 =$

(5) $4 \times 5 + 10 =$

(6) $4 \times 9 + 6 =$

(7) $2 \times 6 - 10 =$

(8) $8 \times 4 + 8 =$

(9) $5 \times 8 - 9 =$

(10) $5 \times 8 + 2 =$

EXERCISE NO. 32

Solve each equation.
Write the solution in the space provided.

(1) $9 \times 4 + 10 =$

(2) $4 \times 2 - 3 =$

(3) $7 \times 6 + 9 =$

(4) $9 \times 4 - 3 =$

(5) $6 \times 7 + 8 =$

(6) $5 \times 9 - 9 =$

(7) $7 \times 6 - 10 =$

(8) $8 \times 10 - 2 =$

(9) $3 \times 5 - 8 =$

(10) $2 \times 8 - 5 =$

EXERCISE NO. 33

Solve each equation.
Write the solution in the space provided.

(1) $8 \times 9 - 8 =$

(2) $7 \times 10 - 9 =$

(3) $3 \times 7 + 8 =$

(4) $7 \times 10 + 7 =$

(5) $7 \times 8 + 4 =$

(6) $6 \times 6 - 8 =$

(7) $7 \times 8 - 8 =$

(8) $6 \times 6 + 5 =$

(9) $9 \times 4 + 8 =$

(10) $3 \times 7 - 3 =$

EXERCISE NO. 34

Solve each equation.
Write the solution in the space provided.

(1) $9 \times 5 + 7 =$

(2) $5 \times 7 + 6 =$

(3) $6 \times 4 + 4 =$

(4) $3 \times 10 + 5 =$

(5) $3 \times 10 - 3 =$

(6) $5 \times 7 - 2 =$

(7) $10 \times 9 - 4 =$

(8) $8 \times 2 - 3 =$

(9) $3 \times 8 - 2 =$

(10) $7 \times 10 + 8 =$

EXERCISE NO. 35

Solve each equation.
Write the solution in the space provided.

(1) $10 \times 8 + 3 =$

(2) $8 \times 9 + 3 =$

(3) $4 \times 6 + 9 =$

(4) $5 \times 6 + 6 =$

(5) $8 \times 9 - 5 =$

(6) $4 \times 5 + 6 =$

(7) $10 \times 8 - 10 =$

(8) $9 \times 3 - 8 =$

(9) $4 \times 5 - 5 =$

(10) $7 \times 10 + 2 =$

EXERCISE NO. 36

Solve each equation.
Write the solution in the space provided.

(1) $10 \times 7 + 9 =$

(2) $4 \times 5 + 8 =$

(3) $3 \times 6 - 8 =$

(4) $6 \times 9 - 5 =$

(5) $9 \times 10 - 9 =$

(6) $6 \times 9 + 5 =$

(7) $5 \times 8 + 10 =$

(8) $8 \times 4 + 8 =$

(9) $8 \times 4 - 7 =$

(10) $2 \times 3 - 3 =$

EXERCISE NO. 37

Solve each equation.
Write the solution in the space provided.

(1) $3 \times 10 - 6 =$

(2) $3 \times 10 + 10 =$

(3) $9 \times 6 + 10 =$

(4) $3 \times 8 - 10 =$

(5) $7 \times 9 + 6 =$

(6) $5 \times 3 + 8 =$

(7) $6 \times 7 - 2 =$

(8) $8 \times 4 + 4 =$

(9) $6 \times 7 + 5 =$

(10) $10 \times 5 + 10 =$

EXERCISE NO. 38

Solve each equation.
Write the solution in the space provided.

(1) $5 \times 7 + 2 =$

(2) $3 \times 9 - 7 =$

(3) $9 \times 8 - 8 =$

(4) $4 \times 5 - 8 =$

(5) $6 \times 6 + 4 =$

(6) $7 \times 10 + 4 =$

(7) $3 \times 9 + 3 =$

(8) $7 \times 9 - 8 =$

(9) $7 \times 9 + 3 =$

(10) $5 \times 7 - 6 =$

EXERCISE NO. 39

Solve each equation.
Write the solution in the space provided.

(1) $3 \times 10 - 5 =$

(2) $7 \times 6 + 4 =$

(3) $2 \times 7 - 6 =$

(4) $8 \times 5 + 8 =$

(5) $5 \times 2 + 6 =$

(6) $4 \times 4 + 4 =$

(7) $9 \times 3 - 5 =$

(8) $2 \times 7 + 10 =$

(9) $8 \times 5 - 9 =$

(10) $6 \times 9 + 9 =$

EXERCISE NO. 40

Solve each equation.
Write the solution in the space provided.

(1) $4 \times 10 + 3 =$

(2) $8 \times 9 + 10 =$

(3) $6 \times 3 + 8 =$

(4) $2 \times 5 - 9 =$

(5) $10 \times 2 + 9 =$

(6) $7 \times 4 - 6 =$

(7) $9 \times 8 + 5 =$

(8) $5 \times 7 - 8 =$

(9) $5 \times 7 + 3 =$

(10) $9 \times 8 - 2 =$

EXERCISE NO. 41

Solve each equation.
Write the solution in the space provided.

(1) $6 \times 10 + 2 \ =$

(2) $6 \times 3 - 7 \ =$

(3) $5 \times 6 - 5 \ =$

(4) $4 \times 4 + 7 \ =$

(5) $6 \times 10 - 6 \ =$

(6) $7 \times 9 - 8 \ =$

(7) $4 \times 4 - 6 \ =$

(8) $2 \times 8 + 3 \ =$

(9) $7 \times 9 + 3 \ =$

(10) $5 \times 6 + 8 \ =$

EXERCISE NO. 42

Solve each equation.
Write the solution in the space provided.

(1) $9 \times 2 - 6 =$

(2) $5 \times 5 - 6 =$

(3) $6 \times 7 - 10 =$

(4) $2 \times 3 + 9 =$

(5) $4 \times 9 + 3 =$

(6) $6 \times 7 + 9 =$

(7) $6 \times 6 + 4 =$

(8) $4 \times 9 - 6 =$

(9) $5 \times 5 + 3 =$

(10) $3 \times 10 - 3 =$

EXERCISE NO. 43

Solve each equation.
Write the solution in the space provided.

(1) $4 \times 5 + 4 \ =$

(2) $6 \times 9 + 2 \ =$

(3) $9 \times 4 + 5 \ =$

(4) $5 \times 9 + 3 \ =$

(5) $3 \times 8 + 5 \ =$

(6) $5 \times 10 - 4 \ =$

(7) $7 \times 2 - 3 \ =$

(8) $5 \times 10 + 4 \ =$

(9) $10 \times 7 - 4 \ =$

(10) $9 \times 4 - 5 \ =$

EXERCISE NO. 44

Solve each equation.
Write the solution in the space provided.

(1) $3 \times 7 + 2 =$

(2) $3 \times 7 - 8 =$

(3) $9 \times 3 - 6 =$

(4) $8 \times 6 - 9 =$

(5) $9 \times 3 + 6 =$

(6) $2 \times 5 + 10 =$

(7) $10 \times 8 - 7 =$

(8) $2 \times 5 - 6 =$

(9) $4 \times 9 + 3 =$

(10) $4 \times 9 - 8 =$

EXERCISE NO. 45

Solve each equation.
Write the solution in the space provided.

(1) $2 \times 8 + 5 =$

(2) $9 \times 5 - 9 =$

(3) $9 \times 6 + 3 =$

(4) $6 \times 7 + 7 =$

(5) $8 \times 9 + 4 =$

(6) $4 \times 10 + 6 =$

(7) $9 \times 5 + 2 =$

(8) $9 \times 6 - 7 =$

(9) $5 \times 3 + 6 =$

(10) $10 \times 2 - 4 =$

EXERCISE NO. 46

Solve each equation.
Write the solution in the space provided.

(1) $2 \times 9 - 8 =$

(2) $7 \times 5 + 2 =$

(3) $6 \times 7 - 6 =$

(4) $10 \times 8 + 6 =$

(5) $4 \times 6 + 3 =$

(6) $3 \times 2 + 3 =$

(7) $2 \times 9 + 7 =$

(8) $4 \times 6 - 10 =$

(9) $5 \times 3 + 9 =$

(10) $10 \times 8 - 5 =$

EXERCISE NO. 1

(1)	$8 - 4 + 10 \ = \ 14$
(2)	$10 - 7 + 10 \ = \ 13$
(3)	$8 + 5 + 5 \ = \ 18$
(4)	$8 - 4 - 2 \ = \ 2$
(5)	$10 + 8 - 6 \ = \ 12$
(6)	$6 + 9 + 9 \ = \ 24$
(7)	$9 - 5 - 3 \ = \ 1$
(8)	$5 - 4 + 2 \ = \ 3$
(9)	$6 - 3 + 8 \ = \ 11$
(10)	$7 - 2 - 2 \ = \ 3$

EXERCISE NO. 2

(1)	$10 - 9 + 3 \ = \ 4$
(2)	$9 + 2 + 5 \ = \ 16$
(3)	$9 - 6 + 7 \ = \ 10$
(4)	$9 + 2 - 8 \ = \ 3$
(5)	$5 - 3 + 10 \ = \ 12$
(6)	$6 + 5 - 6 \ = \ 5$
(7)	$7 + 8 + 5 \ = \ 20$
(8)	$6 - 2 + 9 \ = \ 13$
(9)	$5 + 9 + 10 \ = \ 24$
(10)	$9 - 2 + 9 \ = \ 16$

EXERCISE NO. 3

(1)	$9 - 4 - 3$	$=$	2
(2)	$5 - 3 + 6$	$=$	8
(3)	$3 + 6 + 4$	$=$	13
(4)	$9 - 4 + 10$	$=$	15
(5)	$10 - 8 + 9$	$=$	11
(6)	$2 + 10 - 4$	$=$	8
(7)	$10 - 5 + 8$	$=$	13
(8)	$9 - 6 + 6$	$=$	9
(9)	$5 + 3 + 5$	$=$	13
(10)	$5 - 2 + 8$	$=$	11

EXERCISE NO. 4

(1)	$8 + 8 - 8$	$=$	8
(2)	$9 - 4 + 5$	$=$	10
(3)	$8 - 2 + 8$	$=$	14
(4)	$9 - 8 + 8$	$=$	9
(5)	$5 + 7 - 2$	$=$	10
(6)	$7 - 6 + 2$	$=$	3
(7)	$3 + 9 + 4$	$=$	16
(8)	$10 - 3 - 4$	$=$	3
(9)	$6 - 4 + 5$	$=$	7
(10)	$4 + 6 + 10$	$=$	20

EXERCISE NO. 5

(1)	$6 + 3 - 2$	$=$	7
(2)	$9 - 5 + 10$	$=$	14
(3)	$10 + 4 - 7$	$=$	7
(4)	$7 - 3 + 4$	$=$	8
(5)	$9 - 2 + 9$	$=$	16
(6)	$2 + 7 - 4$	$=$	5
(7)	$10 - 4 + 2$	$=$	8
(8)	$4 - 2 + 7$	$=$	9
(9)	$4 + 9 - 4$	$=$	9
(10)	$3 + 7 - 2$	$=$	8

EXERCISE NO. 6

(1)	$7 - 4 + 7$	$=$	10
(2)	$9 + 4 + 10$	$=$	23
(3)	$9 + 4 - 8$	$=$	5
(4)	$8 + 3 - 6$	$=$	5
(5)	$3 - 2 + 2$	$=$	3
(6)	$8 - 6 + 10$	$=$	12
(7)	$10 + 6 - 4$	$=$	12
(8)	$10 - 9 + 2$	$=$	3
(9)	$8 - 4 + 7$	$=$	11
(10)	$10 + 6 + 7$	$=$	23

EXERCISE NO. 7

(1) $9 - 2 - 5 = 2$
(2) $5 + 5 + 2 = 12$
(3) $9 + 9 - 6 = 12$
(4) $10 + 4 - 5 = 9$
(5) $7 + 3 + 5 = 15$
(6) $2 + 10 - 10 = 2$
(7) $6 - 3 + 10 = 13$
(8) $8 - 3 - 4 = 1$
(9) $3 + 6 - 5 = 4$
(10) $4 - 2 + 3 = 5$

EXERCISE NO. 8

(1) $9 + 8 + 9 = 26$
(2) $5 + 9 - 3 = 11$
(3) $6 - 4 + 2 = 4$
(4) $5 - 2 + 10 = 13$
(5) $4 + 6 - 4 = 6$
(6) $6 + 5 + 10 = 21$
(7) $8 + 2 - 4 = 6$
(8) $8 - 4 + 2 = 6$
(9) $7 + 7 - 2 = 12$
(10) $5 + 9 + 8 = 22$

EXERCISE NO. 9

(1) $5 + 10 + 7 = 22$
(2) $2 + 6 + 4 = 12$
(3) $3 + 3 + 6 = 12$
(4) $6 + 4 - 6 = 4$
(5) $8 + 6 - 3 = 11$
(6) $8 - 7 + 7 = 8$
(7) $8 + 7 + 6 = 21$
(8) $8 + 7 - 6 = 9$
(9) $3 + 3 - 5 = 1$
(10) $4 + 5 + 5 = 14$

EXERCISE NO. 10

(1) $6 + 3 - 5 = 4$
(2) $3 + 2 + 6 = 11$
(3) $10 - 4 + 4 = 10$
(4) $5 + 6 + 7 = 18$
(5) $5 + 6 - 7 = 4$
(6) $2 + 4 - 4 = 2$
(7) $10 + 7 + 3 = 20$
(8) $9 + 9 - 9 = 9$
(9) $10 - 4 + 10 = 16$
(10) $7 + 8 + 9 = 24$

(1)	$7 \times 4 + 10 = 38$	(6) $6 \times 8 - 5 = 43$
(2)	$5 \times 10 + 8 = 58$	(7) $10 \times 5 + 8 = 58$
(3)	$2 \times 9 + 8 = 26$	(8) $10 \times 5 - 8 = 42$
(4)	$5 \times 10 - 7 = 43$	(9) $2 \times 9 - 6 = 12$
(5)	$7 \times 4 - 10 = 18$	(10) $3 \times 2 + 2 = 8$

(1)	$9 \times 8 + 4 = 76$	(6) $9 \times 8 - 9 = 63$
(2)	$9 \times 6 + 9 = 63$	(7) $10 \times 7 - 2 = 68$
(3)	$6 \times 9 - 8 = 46$	(8) $5 \times 10 + 7 = 57$
(4)	$2 \times 5 + 3 = 13$	(9) $8 \times 6 + 2 = 50$
(5)	$10 \times 7 + 8 = 78$	(10) $4 \times 3 - 5 = 7$

(1)	$9 \times 4 - 6 = 30$	(6) $6 \times 9 - 10 = 44$
(2)	$7 \times 8 - 9 = 47$	(7) $4 \times 6 - 2 = 22$
(3)	$8 \times 5 + 4 = 44$	(8) $3 \times 3 - 3 = 6$
(4)	$10 \times 7 + 9 = 79$	(9) $7 \times 8 + 7 = 63$
(5)	$10 \times 7 - 2 = 68$	(10) $4 \times 6 + 2 = 26$

(1)	$3 \times 7 + 6 = 27$	(6) $7 \times 6 - 7 = 35$
(2)	$4 \times 9 + 4 = 40$	(7) $8 \times 5 + 7 = 47$
(3)	$6 \times 4 - 10 = 14$	(8) $4 \times 9 - 9 = 27$
(4)	$2 \times 3 + 2 = 8$	(9) $6 \times 8 - 8 = 40$
(5)	$10 \times 2 - 9 = 11$	(10) $7 \times 6 + 3 = 45$

EXERCISE NO. 15

(1) $9 \times 5 - 9 = 36$

(2) $2 \times 3 - 5 = 1$

(3) $3 \times 4 - 9 = 3$

(4) $7 \times 2 - 7 = 7$

(5) $3 \times 4 + 6 = 18$

(6) $4 \times 9 - 2 = 34$

(7) $10 \times 5 + 10 = 60$

(8) $5 \times 8 - 6 = 34$

(9) $10 \times 5 - 2 = 48$

(10) $4 \times 9 + 4 = 40$

EXERCISE NO. 16

(1) $5 \times 5 + 4 = 29$

(2) $9 \times 3 + 8 = 35$

(3) $6 \times 8 + 3 = 51$

(4) $8 \times 4 + 4 = 36$

(5) $3 \times 9 + 6 = 33$

(6) $3 \times 9 - 9 = 18$

(7) $7 \times 6 + 9 = 51$

(8) $5 \times 7 + 3 = 38$

(9) $4 \times 10 + 3 = 43$

(10) $10 \times 2 + 3 = 23$

EXERCISE NO. 17

(1) $7 \times 2 - 9 = 5$

(2) $5 \times 3 - 4 = 11$

(3) $6 \times 10 + 8 = 68$

(4) $3 \times 5 - 10 = 5$

(5) $5 \times 10 + 8 = 58$

(6) $2 \times 4 + 5 = 13$

(7) $5 \times 3 + 6 = 21$

(8) $6 \times 10 - 7 = 53$

(9) $3 \times 5 + 10 = 25$

(10) $4 \times 6 + 5 = 29$

EXERCISE NO. 18

(1) $3 \times 10 - 3 = 27$

(2) $6 \times 4 + 7 = 31$

(3) $9 \times 6 - 10 = 44$

(4) $7 \times 2 + 5 = 19$

(5) $5 \times 3 - 5 = 10$

(6) $4 \times 5 + 2 = 22$

(7) $10 \times 9 - 6 = 84$

(8) $2 \times 8 + 8 = 24$

(9) $4 \times 5 - 7 = 13$

(10) $5 \times 5 + 10 = 35$

(1) $6 \times 8 - 7 = 41$
(2) $6 \times 8 + 5 = 53$
(3) $10 \times 7 - 3 = 67$
(4) $4 \times 3 + 4 = 16$
(5) $7 \times 9 + 2 = 65$
(6) $3 \times 10 + 6 = 36$
(7) $9 \times 4 + 5 = 41$
(8) $5 \times 5 + 3 = 28$
(9) $10 \times 7 + 7 = 77$
(10) $4 \times 3 - 6 = 6$

(1) $6 \times 3 - 2 = 16$
(2) $10 \times 10 + 8 = 108$
(3) $9 \times 2 + 9 = 27$
(4) $4 \times 2 + 10 = 18$
(5) $8 \times 4 - 7 = 25$
(6) $6 \times 3 + 3 = 21$
(7) $7 \times 5 + 6 = 41$
(8) $5 \times 7 - 4 = 31$
(9) $9 \times 2 - 7 = 11$
(10) $3 \times 8 - 3 = 21$

(1) $9 \times 4 - 8 = 28$
(2) $8 \times 5 - 8 = 32$
(3) $10 \times 2 - 7 = 13$
(4) $3 \times 6 - 10 = 8$
(5) $9 \times 4 + 8 = 44$
(6) $5 \times 8 - 10 = 30$
(7) $4 \times 7 - 7 = 21$
(8) $7 \times 10 - 6 = 64$
(9) $8 \times 5 + 7 = 47$
(10) $10 \times 2 + 4 = 24$

(1) $6 \times 10 - 9 = 51$
(2) $6 \times 10 + 5 = 65$
(3) $3 \times 2 + 10 = 16$
(4) $10 \times 7 - 4 = 66$
(5) $8 \times 4 - 2 = 30$
(6) $9 \times 6 + 9 = 63$
(7) $2 \times 9 - 3 = 15$
(8) $7 \times 8 + 7 = 63$
(9) $7 \times 8 - 7 = 49$
(10) $9 \times 6 - 2 = 52$

(1)	$6 \times 5 + 10$	$=$	40
(2)	$10 \times 10 + 2$	$=$	102
(3)	$8 \times 2 - 5$	$=$	11
(4)	$4 \times 4 + 4$	$=$	20
(5)	$7 \times 9 + 9$	$=$	72
(6)	$10 \times 10 - 6$	$=$	94
(7)	$8 \times 2 + 5$	$=$	21
(8)	$7 \times 5 + 8$	$=$	43
(9)	$4 \times 4 - 3$	$=$	13
(10)	$9 \times 6 + 6$	$=$	60

(1)	$3 \times 8 - 10$	$=$	14
(2)	$3 \times 8 + 2$	$=$	26
(3)	$10 \times 5 + 2$	$=$	52
(4)	$8 \times 2 + 9$	$=$	25
(5)	$9 \times 10 + 3$	$=$	93
(6)	$7 \times 7 + 2$	$=$	51
(7)	$2 \times 9 + 5$	$=$	23
(8)	$4 \times 4 + 5$	$=$	21
(9)	$5 \times 3 + 5$	$=$	20
(10)	$6 \times 6 + 2$	$=$	38

(1)	$5 \times 9 + 2$	$=$	47
(2)	$2 \times 2 + 7$	$=$	11
(3)	$9 \times 6 - 10$	$=$	44
(4)	$7 \times 3 - 7$	$=$	14
(5)	$6 \times 10 + 7$	$=$	67
(6)	$3 \times 8 + 3$	$=$	27
(7)	$5 \times 9 - 9$	$=$	36
(8)	$9 \times 6 + 4$	$=$	58
(9)	$10 \times 4 - 4$	$=$	36
(10)	$6 \times 10 - 5$	$=$	55

(1)	$7 \times 6 - 4$	$=$	38
(2)	$2 \times 2 + 6$	$=$	10
(3)	$10 \times 7 + 10$	$=$	80
(4)	$5 \times 5 - 9$	$=$	16
(5)	$9 \times 4 + 9$	$=$	45
(6)	$6 \times 9 + 9$	$=$	63
(7)	$3 \times 8 + 5$	$=$	29
(8)	$7 \times 6 + 2$	$=$	44
(9)	$10 \times 7 - 6$	$=$	64
(10)	$9 \times 4 - 7$	$=$	29

EXERCISE NO. 27

(1) $2 \times 6 + 4 = 16$
(2) $3 \times 9 + 4 = 31$
(3) $9 \times 8 - 7 = 65$
(4) $6 \times 2 + 5 = 17$
(5) $6 \times 2 - 9 = 3$
(6) $10 \times 3 + 7 = 37$
(7) $3 \times 9 - 9 = 18$
(8) $8 \times 4 + 8 = 40$
(9) $9 \times 8 + 4 = 76$
(10) $5 \times 10 + 2 = 52$

EXERCISE NO. 28

(1) $8 \times 10 + 6 = 86$
(2) $10 \times 7 - 5 = 65$
(3) $10 \times 7 + 3 = 73$
(4) $5 \times 6 + 2 = 32$
(5) $3 \times 3 - 3 = 6$
(6) $9 \times 9 - 3 = 78$
(7) $8 \times 10 - 3 = 77$
(8) $5 \times 2 - 8 = 2$
(9) $5 \times 2 + 5 = 15$
(10) $5 \times 6 - 3 = 27$

EXERCISE NO. 29

(1) $2 \times 8 + 10 = 26$
(2) $4 \times 7 + 4 = 32$
(3) $8 \times 2 - 9 = 7$
(4) $7 \times 5 - 6 = 29$
(5) $6 \times 10 + 4 = 64$
(6) $3 \times 4 - 2 = 10$
(7) $6 \times 3 - 6 = 12$
(8) $7 \times 5 + 3 = 38$
(9) $2 \times 8 - 4 = 12$
(10) $9 \times 6 - 2 = 52$

EXERCISE NO. 30

(1) $5 \times 8 + 5 = 45$
(2) $3 \times 6 + 5 = 23$
(3) $5 \times 8 - 9 = 31$
(4) $10 \times 9 - 2 = 88$
(5) $2 \times 7 + 7 = 21$
(6) $9 \times 10 + 3 = 93$
(7) $6 \times 4 - 5 = 19$
(8) $9 \times 10 - 2 = 88$
(9) $3 \times 6 - 3 = 15$
(10) $2 \times 7 - 2 = 12$

EXERCISE NO. 31

(1) $6 \times 10 + 6 = 66$
(2) $9 \times 7 - 8 = 55$
(3) $4 \times 9 - 7 = 29$
(4) $6 \times 10 - 4 = 56$
(5) $4 \times 5 + 10 = 30$
(6) $4 \times 9 + 6 = 42$
(7) $2 \times 6 - 10 = 2$
(8) $8 \times 4 + 8 = 40$
(9) $5 \times 8 - 9 = 31$
(10) $5 \times 8 + 2 = 42$

EXERCISE NO. 32

(1) $9 \times 4 + 10 = 46$
(2) $4 \times 2 - 3 = 5$
(3) $7 \times 6 + 9 = 51$
(4) $9 \times 4 - 3 = 33$
(5) $6 \times 7 + 8 = 50$
(6) $5 \times 9 - 9 = 36$
(7) $7 \times 6 - 10 = 32$
(8) $8 \times 10 - 2 = 78$
(9) $3 \times 5 - 8 = 7$
(10) $2 \times 8 - 5 = 11$

EXERCISE NO. 33

(1) $8 \times 9 - 8 = 64$
(2) $7 \times 10 - 9 = 61$
(3) $3 \times 7 + 8 = 29$
(4) $7 \times 10 + 7 = 77$
(5) $7 \times 8 + 4 = 60$
(6) $6 \times 6 - 8 = 28$
(7) $7 \times 8 - 8 = 48$
(8) $6 \times 6 + 5 = 41$
(9) $9 \times 4 + 8 = 44$
(10) $3 \times 7 - 3 = 18$

EXERCISE NO. 34

(1) $9 \times 5 + 7 = 52$
(2) $5 \times 7 + 6 = 41$
(3) $6 \times 4 + 4 = 28$
(4) $3 \times 10 + 5 = 35$
(5) $3 \times 10 - 3 = 27$
(6) $5 \times 7 - 2 = 33$
(7) $10 \times 9 - 4 = 86$
(8) $8 \times 2 - 3 = 13$
(9) $3 \times 8 - 2 = 22$
(10) $7 \times 10 + 8 = 78$

EXERCISE NO. 35

(1) $10 \times 8 + 3 = 83$
(2) $8 \times 9 + 3 = 75$
(3) $4 \times 6 + 9 = 33$
(4) $5 \times 6 + 6 = 36$
(5) $8 \times 9 - 5 = 67$
(6) $4 \times 5 + 6 = 26$
(7) $10 \times 8 - 10 = 70$
(8) $9 \times 3 - 8 = 19$
(9) $4 \times 5 - 5 = 15$
(10) $7 \times 10 + 2 = 72$

EXERCISE NO. 36

(1) $10 \times 7 + 9 = 79$
(2) $4 \times 5 + 8 = 28$
(3) $3 \times 6 - 8 = 10$
(4) $6 \times 9 - 5 = 49$
(5) $9 \times 10 - 9 = 81$
(6) $6 \times 9 + 5 = 59$
(7) $5 \times 8 + 10 = 50$
(8) $8 \times 4 + 8 = 40$
(9) $8 \times 4 - 7 = 25$
(10) $2 \times 3 - 3 = 3$

EXERCISE NO. 37

(1) $3 \times 10 - 6 = 24$
(2) $3 \times 10 + 10 = 40$
(3) $9 \times 6 + 10 = 64$
(4) $3 \times 8 - 10 = 14$
(5) $7 \times 9 + 6 = 69$
(6) $5 \times 3 + 8 = 23$
(7) $6 \times 7 - 2 = 40$
(8) $8 \times 4 + 4 = 36$
(9) $6 \times 7 + 5 = 47$
(10) $10 \times 5 + 10 = 60$

EXERCISE NO. 38

(1) $5 \times 7 + 2 = 37$
(2) $3 \times 9 - 7 = 20$
(3) $9 \times 8 - 8 = 64$
(4) $4 \times 5 - 8 = 12$
(5) $6 \times 6 + 4 = 40$
(6) $7 \times 10 + 4 = 74$
(7) $3 \times 9 + 3 = 30$
(8) $7 \times 9 - 8 = 55$
(9) $7 \times 9 + 3 = 66$
(10) $5 \times 7 - 6 = 29$

EXERCISE NO. 39

(1) $3 \times 10 - 5 = 25$
(2) $7 \times 6 + 4 = 46$
(3) $2 \times 7 - 6 = 8$
(4) $8 \times 5 + 8 = 48$
(5) $5 \times 2 + 6 = 16$
(6) $4 \times 4 + 4 = 20$
(7) $9 \times 3 - 5 = 22$
(8) $2 \times 7 + 10 = 24$
(9) $8 \times 5 - 9 = 31$
(10) $6 \times 9 + 9 = 63$

EXERCISE NO. 40

(1) $4 \times 10 + 3 = 43$
(2) $8 \times 9 + 10 = 82$
(3) $6 \times 3 + 8 = 26$
(4) $2 \times 5 - 9 = 1$
(5) $10 \times 2 + 9 = 29$
(6) $7 \times 4 - 6 = 22$
(7) $9 \times 8 + 5 = 77$
(8) $5 \times 7 - 8 = 27$
(9) $5 \times 7 + 3 = 38$
(10) $9 \times 8 - 2 = 70$

EXERCISE NO. 41

(1) $6 \times 10 + 2 = 62$
(2) $6 \times 3 - 7 = 11$
(3) $5 \times 6 - 5 = 25$
(4) $4 \times 4 + 7 = 23$
(5) $6 \times 10 - 6 = 54$
(6) $7 \times 9 - 8 = 55$
(7) $4 \times 4 - 6 = 10$
(8) $2 \times 8 + 3 = 19$
(9) $7 \times 9 + 3 = 66$
(10) $5 \times 6 + 8 = 38$

EXERCISE NO. 42

(1) $9 \times 2 - 6 = 12$
(2) $5 \times 5 - 6 = 19$
(3) $6 \times 7 - 10 = 32$
(4) $2 \times 3 + 9 = 15$
(5) $4 \times 9 + 3 = 39$
(6) $6 \times 7 + 9 = 51$
(7) $6 \times 6 + 4 = 40$
(8) $4 \times 9 - 6 = 30$
(9) $5 \times 5 + 3 = 28$
(10) $3 \times 10 - 3 = 27$

EXERCISE NO. 43

(1) $4 \times 5 + 4 = 24$
(2) $6 \times 9 + 2 = 56$
(3) $9 \times 4 + 5 = 41$
(4) $5 \times 9 + 3 = 48$
(5) $3 \times 8 + 5 = 29$
(6) $5 \times 10 - 4 = 46$
(7) $7 \times 2 - 3 = 11$
(8) $5 \times 10 + 4 = 54$
(9) $10 \times 7 - 4 = 66$
(10) $9 \times 4 - 5 = 31$

EXERCISE NO. 44

(1) $3 \times 7 + 2 = 23$
(2) $3 \times 7 - 8 = 13$
(3) $9 \times 3 - 6 = 21$
(4) $8 \times 6 - 9 = 39$
(5) $9 \times 3 + 6 = 33$
(6) $2 \times 5 + 10 = 20$
(7) $10 \times 8 - 7 = 73$
(8) $2 \times 5 - 6 = 4$
(9) $4 \times 9 + 3 = 39$
(10) $4 \times 9 - 8 = 28$

EXERCISE NO. 45

(1) $2 \times 8 + 5 = 21$
(2) $9 \times 5 - 9 = 36$
(3) $9 \times 6 + 3 = 57$
(4) $6 \times 7 + 7 = 49$
(5) $8 \times 9 + 4 = 76$
(6) $4 \times 10 + 6 = 46$
(7) $9 \times 5 + 2 = 47$
(8) $9 \times 6 - 7 = 47$
(9) $5 \times 3 + 6 = 21$
(10) $10 \times 2 - 4 = 16$

EXERCISE NO. 46

(1) $2 \times 9 - 8 = 10$
(2) $7 \times 5 + 2 = 37$
(3) $6 \times 7 - 6 = 36$
(4) $10 \times 8 + 6 = 86$
(5) $4 \times 6 + 3 = 27$
(6) $3 \times 2 + 3 = 9$
(7) $2 \times 9 + 7 = 25$
(8) $4 \times 6 - 10 = 14$
(9) $5 \times 3 + 9 = 24$
(10) $10 \times 8 - 5 = 75$

Visit
BABY PROFESSOR
EDUCATION KIDS
www.BabyProfessorBooks.com
to download Free Baby Professor eBooks
and view our catalog of new and exciting
Children's Books